Katy PERRY

Rebel Dreamer

Publisher and Creative Director: Nick Wells
Project Editors: Polly Prior and Catherine Taylor
Picture Research: Laura Bulbeck, Alex McClean
Art Director and Layout Design: Mike Spender
Digital Design and Production: Chris Herbert

Special thanks to: Stephen Feather, Karen Fitzpatrick

FLAME TREE PUBLISHING
Crabtree Hall, Crabtree Lane
Fulham, London SW6 6TY
United Kingdom

www.flametreepublishing.com

First published 2012

12 14 16 15 13
1 3 5 7 9 10 8 6 4 2

Flame Tree Publishing is part of The Foundry Creative Media Co. Ltd

A CIP record for this book is available from the British Library upon request.

ISBN 978-0-85775-280-2

Printed in China

Katy PERRY

Rebel Dreamer

ALICE HUDSON

FOREWORD: MANGO SAUL, EDITOR, SUGARSCAPE.COM

**FLAME TREE
PUBLISHING**

Contents

Foreword 6

Pop Sensation 8

Something About The Girl 16

Californian Gurl 24

Early Musical Steps 32

Igniting The Light 40

Hard Graft 48

Big Breaks 56

Naughty Or Nice? 64

One of the Boys 72

Road Warrior 80

MTV Darling 88

Style Icon 96

Queen of Social 104

Family Matters 112

More Than A Songbird 120

Further Information 126

Biographies & Picture Credits 128

Foreword

Hello and welcome to the most beautiful hardback you have ever bought.
It will be a good few weeks before you actually 'read' it. That's after you've devoured every awesome picture in the book. Ladies will love the outfits and men will love, well, the pictures of Katy Perry.

Before this foreword gets too saucy, I have to explain a well-known made-up fact. Katheryn Elizabeth Hudson is every man's secret crush. After releasing her single 'I Kissed a Girl', back in 2008, you wouldn't expect anything less than a full-blown man crush on Katy Perry. How could you resist the titillating lyrics, 'I kissed a girl and I liked it'? The single went on to top the charts in more than 20 countries. Of course it did.

Now you've seen the pictures, you'll absorb the fascinating text. How could you ignore it? From Katy Perry's humble beginning as a child only allowed to listen to gospel music, attending Christian schools and camps, to becoming *Billboard* magazine's 51st-bestselling music artist of the 2000–2009 decade, Katy Perry is the definition of musical triumph. And she's only 27!

And there is no sign of Katy Perry's success diminishing. In October 2011, the singer was crowned the first artist to have three songs sell over five million downloads in America. Top that off with a plethora of awards being won in the same year and four Grammy nominations; there is so much more to come from Katy Perry. A lot more…

Mango Saul, Editor, www.sugarscape.com

Pop Sensation

Katy Perry is one of the world's most successful entertainers. Yet the pop princess, style icon and social-media pioneer has grafted harder than most to put out a successful record. A former Christian singer, Perry's first gospel/rock album sold just 200 copies before the label went bust. Perry moved on, only to be signed and dropped twice over the following six years.

Perry's first commercially successful record was *One of the Boys* (2008). It has since sold over five million copies, the first two singles ('I Kissed A Girl' and 'Hot n Cold') gaining the singer an entry into the *2010 Guinness Book of World Records* for shifting more than two million downloads. Perry's latest release, *Teenage Dream* (2010), has made even bigger waves. May 2011 saw the singer become the first artist in history to spend 52 consecutive weeks in the Top 10 of the *Billboard* Hot 100. She is also only the second artist in the chart's 53-year history to produce five No.1 singles from the same album. Michael Jackson's *Bad* (1987) is the only other album to have achieved the same feat.

Reaping The Awards

Quirky pop princess Perry has more than 60 awards and 200 nominations to her name. In 2008, she won Best New Act at the MTV Europe Music Awards, while in 2009 she was named Best International Female Artist at the BRIT Awards. In 2010, the star took the Best Video gong at the MTV Europe Music

'I don't take anything for granted. There are 500 other girls right behind me. And I know that, because I was one of them.'

Katy Perry

KATY PERRY: REBEL DREAMER

Awards for 'California Gurls' while *Cosmopolitan* magazine named her Ultimate Star of International Music at its Women of the Year awards. She won three gongs at the MTV Video Music Awards in 2011, and was named Favourite Female Singer by Nickelodeon Kids' Choice Awards, and Favourite Female Artist by People's Choice the same year.

A Grammy had failed to materialize as of 2011, though the star had received six nominations. Since her career took off at pace in 2008, Perry has collected six nominations for the American Music Awards, three People's Choice gongs from seven nominations, and four Teen Choice Awards from 17 nominations. She has accolades from as far afield as Japan and Australia.

'I have to appreciate every day, every opportunity, work hard, and continue to evolve as an artist.'

Katy Perry

Media Darling

As Perry's star has risen, so has her public profile. Perry has appeared on dozens of magazine covers around the world, most notably *Rolling Stone*, *Vanity Fair* and *Harper's Bazaar*.

She has also hosted and performed at awards ceremonies including the 53rd Annual Grammy Awards in 2011 and 2008's MTV Europe Music Awards. Perry has made guest appearances on *The Oprah Winfrey Show*, *Ellen*, *Saturday Night Live*, MTV's *America's Best Dance Crew*, *Just Dance 2*, *American Idol* and *Extreme Makeover Home Edition*. She was also a popular guest judge on the UK's *X-Factor*. Unlike some celebrities, Perry manages to come across as genuine, frank and open during interviews, which only adds to her unique charm.

Money And Fame

Perry's runaway commercial success has catapulted her into the realm of the super-rich, at least as far as entertainers are concerned. In 2011, aged 26, Perry was named the eighth highest paid female showbiz star in the world by *Forbes*. Her annual income (before tax) was believed to be US$44 million.

Perry's inclusion on the list indicates she has business smarts. She is unafraid of diversifying her 'brand' as lucrative contracts with skin care brand Proactiv, sports giant Adidas, and *Just Dance* video game producer Ubisoft demonstrate. Perry has even moved into cosmetics, her first fragrance Purr winning an award for 'Best New Celebrity Fragrance' at the 2011 UK FiFi Awards and, more importantly, flying off shelves.

A separate *Forbes* list, the 'Celebrity 100', measures money and fame via a series of categories. While Perry was only 38th for 'money,' and 20th for 'TV/radio', her rank of 4th in 'social' and 3rd in 'web' categories pulled the starlet up to an impressive 12th in the overall list.

'I wouldn't be working at this pace now if I didn't know that fame is truly fleeting.'

Katy Perry

> '*It just got to the point where nobody knew what to do anymore. They had tried so many different things. Nothing had worked. So eventually, everybody realized that it was time to move on.*'

> *Angelica Cob-Baehler*

> '*I feel like I can pave my own path.*'

> *Katy Perry*

Something About The Girl

While a fan of candy floss, girly colours and cats, Perry has always had a rebellious streak. To this day, she is unafraid of letting the rebel in her show. Despite an über-strict Christian upbringing, Perry has happily cultivated an increasingly sexy image. She has no qualms wearing the tiniest of outfits, appears lying naked on a pink cloud for the cover of her second album *Teenage Dream*, and even posed semi-nude for *Rolling Stone*. The rebel in Perry extends to her songs. She has always written her own material, in which an irreverent, playful sense of humour is apparent. Not everyone finds her funny, however. She first rocked the conservative boat with 'Ur So Gay' and then created a storm of controversy – and extra publicity – with the 'bi-curious' hit 'I Kissed a Girl'. Perry appears relatively unconcerned with self-censorship. She sometimes swears during interviews (although she never takes the Lord's name in vain). Even Perry's marriage could be perceived as rebellious. Husband Russell Brand is no choirboy, but a self-confessed former heroin and sex addict.

Sense And Sensibility

Despite deviating from what her devout parents consider appropriate, Perry has an excellent track record as a

focused professional. Unlike many starlets, she has yet to hit the headlines for something embarrassing or illegal. No public meltdowns, no reported issues with drink or drugs, no sex tapes, no arrests. While her songs have caused an uproar, Perry the person is refreshingly scandal free. Unlike her husband in his wild days, Perry says 'casual sex grosses me out'. In many ways she upholds the core Christian family values instilled in her as a child. While it would be wrong to call Perry boring, the singer's complete dedication to her craft is apparent. It would seem a screwed-on head, coupled with talent, ambition and endless determination, has helped her carve out a career any pop princess would be proud of.

Katy Cats

Perry has a seemingly natural ability to connect with her fans, particularly online. Besides singing, songwriting and performing, 'buzz generation' is up there among her greatest strengths. Not only does Perry communicate with fans through her lyrics – she is also a prolific user of social networks. The singer has affectionately dubbed die-hard fans 'Katy Cats' – a global troupe of mainly young girls and teenagers. Katy Cats worship Perry for her colourful style, glossy image, catchy tunes and spunky attitude. And the business-savvy star never tires of coming up with new and innovative ways of engaging with her adoring public. From gimmicks such as making album covers – or a concert

'I don't end up wasted with my face down in an alleyway. I steer the ship pretty good so I don't hit any icebergs.'

Katy Perry

venue – smell like candy floss, to a myriad of carefully planned online teasers for her videos and even the creation of an entire online alter ego, Perry's attention to detail shows she is as dedicated to the business side of her job as she is to her craft.

Caring and Sharing

Katy Perry has no problem sharing her every move online. This is a big bonus for a celebrity living in an increasingly digital and social media-centred world. Perry keeps up a constant stream of cyber chatter via her blog and Twitter, in particular. Fans never have to wait long to hear from Perry. On her recent California Dreams Tour, Perry took fans (virtually) backstage, posting a series of clips of her showing them what goes on behind the scenes.

Before a new single is released, Perry will tease with short previews of artwork and videos. She often runs competitions to further get fans involved. To coincide with the release of the inspirational single 'Firework', for example, fans were invited to send in short videos of them talking about a 'Firework' or inspirational person they knew, with Perry posting the best entries on her blog and other channels.

With a constant stream of social content keeping her fans engaged and wanting more, it is no wonder Perry's Katy Cats were nominated for the MTV O Music Awards Fan Army award.

Californian Gurl

Katy Perry was born Katheryn Elizabeth Hudson in California on 25 October 1984. She has an older sister named Angela and a younger brother, David. Both parents are evangelical pastors who operated a 'travelling ministry' when the children were young. This meant Katy moved seven times between the ages of three and 11, when the family settled in Santa Barbara, California. Young Katy's upbringing was unusual in many ways due to her parents' fanatical devotion to religion. In other respects, however, it was typically Californian. Perry says she has fond memories of long days spent outdoors in the Californian sun. The beach was her playground. 'I tried to be a bit like the typical Californian girl,' she told *E! True Hollywood Story*. 'I tried to surf – I wasn't very good.' Perry had better luck with rollerblading and skateboarding, which she took up about age 13. She says she was 'really involved' in the skateboard culture popular at the time. David Hudson, Katy's younger brother, says she was a bit of a 'tom boy' while they were growing up. The 'rough and tumble' young Katy Hudson showed no early signs of morphing into an ultra-groomed, girly pop princess.

'Katy was kind of like a brother to me, she would be so rugged and just wouldn't care.' David Hudson

Strictly, Restrictedly Bizarre

Perry's award-winning music videos feature constantly on MTV, which is ironic, considering the music channel was blocked from the Hudson household while Katy was growing up. In fact, just about all magazines, movies and television were off-limits to the Hudson kids. Bedtime stories were passages from the Bible. Non-Christian music was not allowed in the house. Even the cartoon *The Smurfs* – the big-screen version of which Perry stars in – was considered unacceptable. Perry's folks believed it contained too much sorcery and magic. The rules the Hudsons enforced during Perry's childhood demonstrate the God-fearing, fire-and-brimstone nature of their beliefs. Perry was brought up to believe in Satan as a real being. To this day, she admits getting seriously scared in disaster movies due to the apocalypse scenarios she was told as a child. The mentality even extended to the actual eating of food: devilled eggs had to be renamed 'angeled eggs' while the sweets 'Lucky Charms' simply were not allowed. The word 'lucky' was completely banned; Katy's mother said it reminded her of 'Lucifer'.

Preaching Parents

Perry's parents, Keith and Mary Hudson, weren't always God-fearing. Both are born-again Christians who came to the church later in life. Both have intriguing pasts. Keith Hudson is a former LSD-using hippy who used to play tambourine with

'*I didn't have a childhood. I come from a very non-accepting family, but I'm very accepting.*'

Katy Perry

Sly and the Family Stone. His life changed abruptly 40 years ago, when, alone in an apple orchard at night, visions of Bible passages appeared before his eyes.

Perry's mother is a former wild child who once hung out with Jimi Hendrix. She married a one-legged former race-car driver and relocated to Zimbabwe, although after that marriage ended, she returned to the US, becoming a news reporter. Covering a Christian tent revival one day, Mary found God, and Keith Hudson, at the same time. Together they shunned the secular world and tried to protect their children from it. Perry says that when growing up her father often spoke in tongues, while her mother interpreted. 'Speaking in tongues is as normal to me as "pass the salt",' Katy told *Rolling Stone*.

'We get people all the time saying 'How? How, that you're a minister all these years and you raised Katy in the Church, how could she come out with a song like that?' I look at them and I say, 'I don't know'." *Keith Hudson*

'She has *always* been our *songbird.*'

Katy's elder sister, Angela

'*All* the *walls* come *down* in my *songs.*'

Katy Perry

Early Musical Steps

When Perry was nine years old, her sister Angela started having singing lessons. Perry, who describes herself as a 'typical middle child' naturally wanted to copy everything Angela did. So, she routinely stole her sister's practice cassette tapes (all gospel), when Angela wasn't home. She would then put them in her own tape deck and sing along to them herself.

One day, she showed off to her mother who, recognizing the talent, suggested her younger daughter better get voice lessons too. Looking back, Angela says Katy was always singing, even singing herself and the other children to sleep. The family dubbed her 'Katy Bird' due to her love of warbling. Katy remembers singing being an attention-grabbing exercise on her part. 'It was the one thing I could pull out and everyone would just pay attention and drop what they were doing. It felt like I had some kind of power, in a way.'

Gospel And Guitar

About the same time she began vocal coaching, the young songbird began showing off her talents in church. She loved performing. The whole idea got even better when Keith Hudson began paying his daughter $10 to sing at family functions. Perry says, '$10 is a lot of money when you're nine years old.' The aspiring musician also began busking twice a week at the local farmers' market. Her confidence as a performer was obvious even then. A video of one of the gigs

sees her happily ad-libbing to the crowds between songs, telling them, sweetly, and with a big smile, that: 'If you don't live your life for Christ – I'm just going to say it – life is pretty empty, and, well, there may be no reason to live at all.' Perry got her first guitar aged 13. She found it immediately empowering and began writing her own songs.

'This is, like, *ammo*. Being able to say *what I think* and put it on a bed of music. *Wow*…it made me feel, just like, *magical.*'

Katy Perry on discovering the guitar.

Swing Influence

Perry had another extra-curricular activity as a child – she took swing dance lessons including Lindy Hop and The Jitterbug. It is here she says her love of 1940s fashion hails back to. The star says she was 'in awe' of the older dancers, in particular their dedication to the whole era, especially when it came to fashion. 'From the moment they stepped out of their old Chevy to the minute their foot hit the ground, they were head-to-toe from a time warp,' recalls Perry. 'They had an attitude, they had an air, they were unforgettable.' She credits those dance

lessons at the Santa Barbara Recreation Center with inspiring her trademark vintage style – it was the pencil skirts, tight cardigans and bullet bras which really caught the young Perry's imagination. 'It was so unique and different than what was going on in the 2000s.'

'I really like to look like a history book.'

Katy Perry on her vintage style.

High School Drop-Out

Perry attended Dos Pueblos High School in Goleta, California, an affluent school with a proud history in American football. As she was not allowed to attend parties or school dances, and was opted out of sex education classes, Perry stood out a little, but while she wasn't necessarily part of the 'in' crowd, neither was the church singer a nerd. 'I was a hop-around,' she says. 'I hung out with the rockabilly crew, the guys who were trying to be rappers, the funny kids,' At 15, country rock veterans Steve Thomas and Jennifer Knapp from the gospel scene in Nashville, Tennessee, spotted Perry singing in church. They invited her to spend time with them in 'Music City' honing her craft. With her dreams now firmly set on a career in music, and with her parents' approval – they by now considered her talent a 'gift from God' – Perry dropped out of high school. She enrolled in the Music Academy of the West in Santa Barbara (and studied Italian opera for a short time) while her parents patiently ferried her to and from Nashville.

'It was always obvious that she would be successful. Katy is talented, and could command attention in a room even before she was famous.'

Shannon Woodward, childhood friend and Raising Hope actress.

Igniting The Light

Perry sang in church between the ages of nine and 17. Gospel was a huge influence musically. Yet despite the Hudsons' ban on pop music, it was impossible to protect young Perry's precious ears 24/7. The Hudson children were allowed to visit friends' houses and Katy – although she still enjoyed penning religious-themed tunes – began to harbour a secret love for pop and rock culture. 'I was Christian but modern,' she says of her early musical style. Whenever she went to a friend's house she would immediately switch on MTV. She was hooked. Perry has often described herself at that time as a 'sponge', soaking up life, pop culture particularly. She also began to realize that she didn't have to agree with everything her parents said. Letting go was 'a process', she says. 'I was so open to new experiences.'

Musical Influences

Perry says she constantly thinks about music. 'My brain never turns off.' She carries a notebook with her at all times in case lyrical inspiration strikes. She also has a voice recorder to preserve precious melodies that pop into her head.

Of the artists that inspire her, it was Freddie Mercury who would make the biggest impression on young Perry. While listening to 'banned' music one day with a girlfriend, she heard Queen for the first time. 'Time stood still,' she recalls. 'The music was totally different from anything I'd heard.'

'I became a sponge for all that I had missed – the music, the movies. I was as curious as the cat.'

Katy Perry

Mercury's flamboyant, fun and cheeky lyrics appealed to Perry's fun-loving personality. 'He seemed to have come on stage like a firecracker. And I love that. He was an entertainer. You know? And that's what I want to be, an entertainer.'

'The heavens opened my eyes when I stumbled upon a Queen record and I was forever saved.'

Katy Perry

Girl Power

With their girl-power attitude, artists Alanis Morissette and Gwen Stefani also had a big impact on the teenage Perry. Songs such as Morissette's 'You Oughta Know' and Stefani's 'Just A Girl' made an impression. Later, Perry would handpick Morissette's producer, Glen Ballard, as someone she wanted to work with. Perry also names The Beach Boys, Heart, Joni Mitchell, Paul Simon, Imogen Heap, Rufus Wainwright and Madonna as other key early musical influences. Artists she admires today include Lady Gaga, Rihanna, Sia, Beth Ditto, Ellie Goulding and Marina & the Diamonds – the latter two

have opened for her shows. Perry also expresses admiration for Ke$ha, whom she has known 'for ever,' since they were both 'just hustling' in Los Angeles. 'She's actually in the "I Kissed a Girl" video,' reveals Perry.

'It inspires me to see girls conquer.'

Katy Perry

Pious Perry

Perry has spoken frankly of her disapproval of aspects of her parents' beliefs. A focus on fear and fire and brimstone, coupled with intolerance of other people, affected her childhood. 'I knew about Hell from the moment I understood a sentence. I had felt boards with Satan and people gnashing their teeth,' recalls Perry. Despite her parents' best efforts, Perry claims she never bought into the 'rules and hatred' that she says are part and parcel of their religious beliefs.

Perhaps surprisingly, she has not completely cut religious ties. 'I still believe that Jesus is the Son of God. But I also believe in extraterrestrials.' Despite her skimpy clothing, raunchy videos and provocative song lyrics, Perry gets mad if she hears husband Russell Brand blaspheme. She also spoke out publicly against Lady Gaga filming a clip with a rosary in her mouth. Says Perry, 'I think when you put sex and spirituality together in the same bottle and shake it up, bad things happen.'

'I got this Jesus tattoo on my wrist when I was 18 because I know that it's always going to be a part of me. When I play, it's staring right back at me, saying "remember where you come from".'

Katy Perry

'There were **months** that *turned* into years that *Katy* was **struggling** in *LA* not being able to get her **voice across** and, very *frustrated*, but she **never** gave up.'

Bradford Cobb, manager

> '*I gave myself until I turned 25 to make it. And if it didn't happen, I thought I'd just try to find a nice husband.*'
>
> *Katy Perry*

Hard Graft

Perry's journey to musical stardom would be long and arduous. While the curious teenager was already interested in pop culture and had begun penning lyrics about boys, outwardly, her subject material remained strictly Christian.

She signed her first record deal, with Christian label Red Hill Records, aged 15. The LP *Katy Hudson* was released in 2001. 'Trust in Me' was the lead single, the genre gospel rock. Perry is credited solely for writing four tracks, and is co-writer on the remaining six. Unfortunately for Perry, the album was a complete flop and the label went bust soon after its release. The singer did at least receive one glowing review: *Christianity Today* called her 'a remarkable young talent' and 'gifted songwriter' and predicted she would 'go far' in the business. Little did they know in what direction.

Island Def Jam

Perry re-focused on California, adopting her mother's maiden name to avoid confusion with Hollywood actress, Kate Hudson. The determined young woman soon had another deal, signing with Island Def Jam Music Group. She was ready to leave gospel/rock behind. An Island employee asked what producer she would choose to work with, if she could choose.

Perry had no idea but that night saw Glen Ballard being interviewed on TV about his work on Alanis Morissette's *Jagged Little Pill* (1995). Perry expressed interest and a meeting with Ballard was arranged. The producer was instantly won over and the pair would work together in earnest for years. Says Perry of Ballard, 'He taught me even more about songwriting and pushed me artistically until I was like, I can't write another song.' An album was due for release on the Island label yet despite churning out oodles of material, heartbreakingly for Perry, she was dropped before anything happened.

'My vision was really strong and I wasn't prepared to water it down.'

Katy Perry

Road To Nowhere

Convinced of her potential, and with Perry still determined, Ballard took her to Columbia Records. She was signed in 2004, yet the relationship would, yet again, ultimately go nowhere. The star has since complained that the label would not allow her in the 'driver's seat'.

> *'Being let go from your second major label recording contract – it's kind of a big deal.'*
>
> *Angelica Cob-Baehler*

One of Columbia's ideas was to pair Perry up with record production team The Matrix, who were working on an album. While material was recorded, yet again, the project was shelved, although not before Perry caught the attention of the music press. She was named the 'Next Big Thing' by *Blender* magazine while *Teen People* deemed her 'One To Watch'. In the meantime, Perry continued to work hard, holding on to hopes of an album release around the corner. Columbia dropped Perry in 2006.

Rock Bottom

Doubly defeated at being dropped again, Perry became despondent. 'I thought, I shouldn't have gotten my hopes up,' she says. 'I was just sitting there in my car that I was two months behind on payments for, knowing I didn't have money for rent.' Her car was in fact repossessed twice during this difficult time. The struggling singer lived on a diet of baked potatoes, beans and Taco Bell.

The months following the Columbia dumping were the closest she came to getting into real trouble. She started to party more, attempting to drown her sorrows with alcohol. 'I used to just feel numb,' Perry told *Instyle* magazine of her early struggles. 'It was like taking a kid to Disneyland and then making them wait outside. The people just wouldn't let me through the gates – what could I do?'

Big Breaks

Angelica Cob-Baehler met Perry while Cob-Baehler was a publicist at Columbia Records. She accepted a new role at Virgin around the time Perry was being dropped, and recommended Perry enthusiastically, telling her new colleagues: 'You have to meet Katy Perry, she's a star.'

Cob-Baehler first introduced Perry to A&R man Chris Anokute. Together, they went to meet then-chairman of Virgin Records, Jason Flom. While other Virgin executives were not immediately sold on Perry, Flom became convinced she was 'the next big thing'. Prolonged discussions with Columbia eventually secured Virgin the rights to Perry's unfinished album and the frustrated yet relieved star was once more a signed artist. Her deal was with the newly created Capitol Music Group, a merger between Virgin and Capitol. Anokute admits Perry was taken on 'for cheap'. 'It was a really bad deal because she'd been dropped, so it's not like we were going to give her a huge advance.' Most of the album was already written. All Capitol thought it was missing was a sure-fire radio hit. They brought in Lukasz Gottwald, aka Dr Luke, who Perry had already worked with, and Max Martin, to collaborate. Future smash hits, 'I Kissed a Girl' and 'Hot n Cold' were soon born.

Ur So Gay

Perry tested the waters before her album, *One of the Boys*, was finally released. She and her team harnessed the then-fledging power of social media to release the single 'Ur So Gay' as a free download on her Myspace page. The song made waves. About straight guys who are so girly and vain that they really should be gay, the song is typical Perry: light-hearted, teasing and a bit risqué. Perry's kudos went way up when Madonna called the track her 'favourite song right now' while being interviewed by Kiss FM, in Phoenix, Arizona.

Perry later told *Saturday Night* magazine the mention felt particularly special. 'I haven't heard Madonna giving a whole lot of shoutouts. It was nice that she did it at the beginning of my career before anything happened. She kind of gave me a "champagne send-off" and of course it's every girl's dream to have any kind of correlation with the queen.'

'She proceeded to work as hard as any artist has ever worked, relentlessly visiting radio, travelling the world, signing every autograph – she was singularly focused and driven.'

Jason Flom

'There was this energy about her, this charisma, an instant X-factor.'

Angelica Cob-Baehler on Katy Perry

'There is so *much more* to *come*, you just have *no idea* of the range that *Katy Perry* has, *I mean*, the *sky's* the *limit*, truly.'

Glen Ballard

'Cherry Chapstick'

'I Kissed a Girl' launched Katy Perry full-throttle into the world of mainstream pop stardom she had craved for so long. The track's controversial subject matter almost led to catastrophe, however, before it was even released. 'Nobody [at the label] believed in the record,' Chris Anokute has claimed. 'They said, "Who's going to play this in the Bible Belt?" Our head of Top 40 radio, Dennis Reese, was the one that made everybody believe. At that point, we just had to put it out because Katy was on her way to getting dropped again.'

At first some radio stations were hesitant to play it. The song's lyrics include: 'I kissed a girl and I liked it/The taste of her cherry chapstick/I kissed a girl just to try it/Hope my boyfriend don't mind it/It felt so wrong/It felt so right/Don't mean I'm in love tonight' and 'I don't even know your name/It doesn't matter/You're my experimental game/Just human nature/It's not what good girls do/Not how they should behave/My head gets so confused/So hard to obey'. Needless to say, Perry's parents were not impressed.

The first station to pick the single up was The River, in Nashville. Other stations soon followed suit, and got a huge reaction. Used in an episode of popular teen show *Gossip Girl*, the catchy song soon climbed the charts. 'I Kissed a Girl' would go on to spend seven weeks at No. 1 on the *Billboard* Hot 100. It also reached No. 1 on the Mainstream Top 40 chart and went on to top the charts in 30 countries including the UK, Australia and Canada. It has sold over 4 million digital downloads.

Naughty Or Nice?

Perry has never shied away from controversy. She knew as well as anybody that releasing 'Ur So Gay' and 'I Kissed a Girl' would cause a stir. The star remained unperturbed and unapologetic as her motives and values were picked over in the press. She told *Saturday Night* magazine: 'Well I knew I wasn't serving plain ol' vanilla. I knew it had a bit more spice to it! Some people found it provocative, some found it curious and some just realized it was a good ol' fun pop song. I have no agenda but sometimes people overthink things.' Her parents added to the controversy – and press attention – by publicly condemning the song as 'shameful and disgusting' for 'promoting homosexuality'. Hate sites condemning Perry and comparing her with the Devil soon cropped up. She was never worried. 'I never want to be boring, so therefore I aspire to always be interesting, experimental and entertaining. There are many cards in my deck of personality.'

*'There's a **whole other side** of me people didn't know existed.'*

Katy Perry

Lipstick Lesbian?

Not only did Perry get herself in trouble with Bible Belt crusaders, 'Ur So Gay' and 'I Kissed a Girl' also saw criticism levelled at the star from the gay community. Some claimed lyrics such as 'You're so gay and you don't even like boys' were demeaning to homosexuals. 'I am sure Katy would get a critical reception if she expressed comparable sentiments in a song called Ur So Black, Jewish or disabled,' activist Peter Tatchell complained. Perry defended

herself, saying she was merely poking fun at today's 'metrosexual world'. 'I'm not saying you're gay, you're so lame. I'm saying you're so gay, but I don't understand it because you don't like boys!' Others in the gay community thought Perry deserved scorn for her brazen use of 'bi-curiosity' as a marketing ploy. Perry has never said she is bisexual, although she has alluded to having kissed a girl when she was a teenager, and has made headlines talking of 'girl crushes' on Scarlett Johansson and Cheryl Cole, the latter of whom she publicly described as 'edible'.

Press Pressure

Having fought so hard for fame, attention-loving Perry initially coped fine with the sudden intrusion of the paparazzi. 'Cameras and paparazzi and the whole bit – you just have to learn how to breathe and balance,' she says. Since hooking up with comedian Russell Brand, however, media attention has intensified and on occasion has been too much for Perry to bear. In 2010, an incident where the couple were mobbed by shutter-bugs at Los Angeles International Airport ended up with Brand in jail for minor assault. The couple say the photographer was trying to take improper shots. After Brand was released, posting £12,800 bail, angry Perry hotly defended his actions tweeting, 'If you cross the line & try and put a lens up my dress, my fiancé will do his job & protect me.'

'Sometimes when you are on a rollercoaster ride, you know, it's not fun and you freak out.'

Katy Perry

Celebrity Spats

Outspoken Perry has occasionally ruffled celebrity feathers on her way to the top. Early in her career, she was asked to describe herself and replied that she was 'a skinnier version of Lily Allen'. The UK singer responded by publicly calling Perry 'crass', claiming: 'I know for a fact that she was an American version of me. She was signed by my label in America as "We need to find something controversial and kooky like Lily Allen".' Perry apologized, saying she was 'trying to be funny'. Relations have remained frosty. Perry also had a very public spat with Calvin Harris, an artist she used to only dream of working with 'because he created disco'. Due to open for her in the UK in 2011, Harris cancelled on short notice, due to production concerns. Furious Perry took to Twitter, first letting fans know about the cancellation, then blasting Harris publicly when he tried to explain. 'It's fine, I'm used to you canceling on me, it's become your staple!' she vented. Perry's anger prompted a bizarre response from some of her fans. A clearly astonished Harris later tweeted 'WTF are Katy Perry fans telling me to KILL MYSELF on Twitter for? Seriously. I'm a producer making music. Leave me alone please thanks x'.

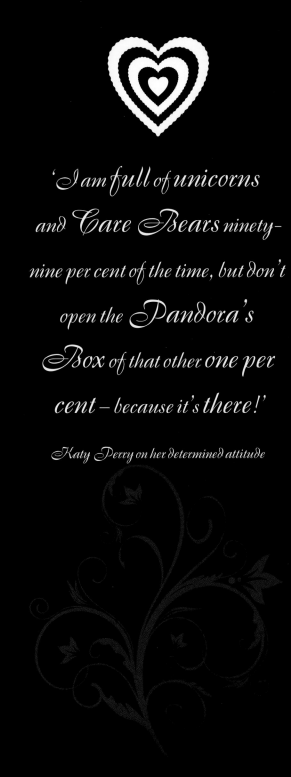

'I am full of unicorns and Care Bears ninety-nine per cent of the time, but don't open the Pandora's Box of that other one per cent – because it's there!'

Katy Perry on her determined attitude

'I think people appreciate a songwriter who shows different sides. The whole angst thing is cool, but if that's all you've got, it's just boring. Everything I write, whether it's happy or sad, has a sense of humour to it.'

Katy Perry

One of the Boys

One of the Boys was released in June 2008. 'I Kissed a Girl' would not be the only track to make an impact. 'Hot n Cold', 'Thinking of You' and 'Waking Up in Vegas' all enjoyed chart success and ensured Perry was not a one-hit wonder. *Boys* was the 33rd bestselling album in the world that year, while in 2009 'I Kissed a Girl' and 'Hot n Cold' were certified three-times platinum for individual sales of over three million each. 'Hot n Cold', which peaked at No. 3 on the *Billboard* chart after its release, has since achieved digital downloads numbering over 5 million, making it the most successful song of Perry's career so far in the US. Perry is named as co-writer on every track, as well as writing three of the songs on her own.

Reviews

One of the Boys scored Perry two Grammy nominations, in 2009 and 2010, yet reviews were decidedly mixed. *Billboard* magazine was definitely in the minority when it gushed that 'not since *Jagged Little Pill* has a debut album been so packed with potential hits'. Many other critics criticized the record for sounding too glossy and over-produced, and that the lyrics lacked substance. *NME* dismissed the album, stating: 'Madonna and Perez Hilton may be fans, but if you've got even a passing interest in actually enjoying a record, don't buy this one.'

'She is *musically* adventurous with a *unique personality* and style that defines her as a *star* for the *next generation*.'

Jason Flom, chair and CEO

of Capitol Music Group

Teenage Dream

Teenage Dream was released in the US in August 2010. An immediate hit, it sold 192,000 copies in its first week and would go on to break records with all five singles reaching No. 1 on all major charts, including digital and airplay. While retaining Perry's trademark candy-coated pop vibe with tracks such as 'California Gurls,' *Dream* also features work with deeper themes, such as the self-esteem boosting power ballad, 'Firework', Perry's favourite track. She describes the feeling of songwriting like an 'anvil lifting' off her chest, and claims she sought inspiration for *Dream* from the 'vibe' of her hometown Santa Barbara and the 'purity' of her childhood. 'My record is like an airplane's black box,' she says. 'That's where all the information is. If you want to know what happened, or what my viewpoints are, it's all right there.'

'When I was touring, I wanted people to dance more. So I wrote an album that made people move, yet didn't sacrifice the story substance that I had on the last record.'

Katy Perry

Pin-Up Girl

Perry says she called the album *Teenage Dream* 'because I feel I always want to be that pin-up poster'. The title track features the lyric: 'You think I'm pretty without any makeup on.' She admits this relates to her relationship with Brand. The album's producers include Glen Ballard (Alanis Morissette, No Doubt), Max Martin, Tricky Stewart, Stargate, Dave Stewart (Eurythmics), Dr Luke (Kelly Clarkson, Avril Lavigne), Butch Walker (Pink), Greg Wells (Mika) and River Cuomo (Weezer). Dr Luke says of working with Perry: 'Katy definitely knows what she wants and doesn't want. She has an amazing voice, great taste and she makes great videos. It's nice to work with an artist who can deliver your music so well.'

'She wasn't going to stop. She had that fighting spirit. She wasn't staying at home, sulking, she was working as hard as anybody. You have to have that with an artist, or you don't have a chance.'

Bradford Cobb, manager

'I wanted to be that quirky girl who writes funny songs that still have meaning.'

Katy Perry

Road Warrior

Before she hit the big-time, Perry opened for acts including Mika, Puffy AmiYumi and The Starting Line. It would be her inclusion on the 2008 Warped Tour bill that would really test her as a performer. Perry was at that time riding high on the success of 'I Kissed a Girl', yet Warped Tour concert-goers didn't fit her teenybopper target audience. Perry's management hoped the Warped Tour would establish Perry as a credible performer and not merely a one-hit wonder. It was hard work. Perry played all 47 dates and had to earn respect from the audience every single night. She did this by employing foot stamping and spitting, and generally blowing the cutesy pop princess thing out of the water. 'I wanted to add Katy because I'd heard her record and knew she had some attitude,' tour founder Kevin Lyman recalls. 'She worked hard every day and became a great live artist.'

'It's going to be an edible-looking tour. It's going to be candy, a smorgasbord.'

Katy Perry on her California Dreams tour.

Hello Katy!

Perry's first headlining tour, in support of her hit record *One of the Boys*, would see her perform 90 dates across four continents between January and November 2009. Called the 'Hello Katy' Tour, it played on the 'Hello Kitty' theme featuring giant images of Perry's beloved pet cat, Kitty Purry.

Perry announced the tour just after the MTV Europe Music Awards in November 2008, which she hosted. Perry was excited to have 'the guy who creates stages for Madonna' working on her tour and let fans know she couldn't wait to indulge her 'obsession with fruit and cats and designing all different outfits'. Hello Katy would go on to almost completely sell out across venues in North America, Europe, Asia and Australia. Support acts included 3OH!3, Beduk, Sliimy and The Daylights.

Candyfornia Dreaming

Perry's aim for her second tour was to make it 'ten times better' than the last. California Dreams, in support of *Teenage Dream*, kicked off in February 2011. It featured 122 dates across Europe, Australasia, Asia and North America, also including, a first for the star, three South American dates.

The singer teased her legions of Twitter followers prior to hitting the road: 'I hope that it's going to engage all of your senses: sight, sound, smell, taste, touch.' The UK leg of the Dreams tour sold out within 30 minutes, while it ranked 21st in

'When they [Katy's parents] realized how much attention it was getting her, they kind of jumped on the band wagon. And Dad was telling everybody that he was Katy Perry's dad.'

Katy's elder sister Angela

'Katy had such strong belief in herself and just kept going. That girl works harder than anybody. And she's so in love with what she's doing.'

Kara Dio Guardi,

American Idol judge

Pollstar's Top 50 Worldwide Tour (Mid-Year), pulling in over US$25 million. The tour received good reviews worldwide. Perry is praised for putting on a sensory overload that comes across almost like a musical rather than just a concert.

Dreams – Show Highlights

The Dreams show is set in Candyland. As Perry takes the audience through her catalogue of hits, the show follows a storyline. Perry is like Alice, or Dorothy, lost in a strange candy world, looking for something – in this case, her giant lilac cat, Kitty Purry, and the love of her life, the Baker's Boy.

The sensory extravaganza sees Perry in 16 different costumes, including seven changes during the song 'Hot n Cold' alone. At one point, theatrical Perry eats a magical brownie that transforms her into a cat woman. At other times, she shares the stage with a human slot machine, showgirls, a pair of mime artists and an Elvis impersonator. There are aerial stunts, laser beams and a massive pink cloud, on top of which Perry belts out 'Thinking of You'.

During 'Last Friday Night (T.G.I.F.)' photos and feedback from fans are displayed on big screens, while Perry finishes the show with 'California Gurls', dressed in a bra shaped like Hershey's Kisses, dancing with a line of gingerbread men and soaking the crowd with a whipped-cream bazooka. The show includes an acoustic medley of covers, including Rihanna's 'Only Girl', and involves crowd interaction as around 20 fans are pulled onstage to dance with Kitty Purry – and Katy Perry.

'*It was* definitely *a challenge for* my parents *to let their seventeen-year-old* daughter *move to* big *L.A.* But they *were* supportive *because they knew that's* where she needed *to be for her* career.'

brother David Hudson

MTV Darling

As Perry's career has progressed, her videos have become increasingly provocative and over the top – as well as hugely successful. In 2008 she received five nominations for the MTV Video Music Awards, though failed to win any. In 2011 she received ten nominations. This was more than any other artist. Perry was also the only singer in history to have four different videos shown in various categories. She took home three gongs: Video of the Year for 'Firework', and Best Collaboration and Best Special Effects for 'E.T.' featuring Kanye West. The pop singer has been able to boost her street cred and extend the range of her MTV fan base by featuring artists including rappers Snoop Dogg, Missy Elliot and Kanye West in her increasingly elaborate and expensive videos.

Snoop Candy

Perry's collaboration with badass rapper Snoop Dogg seems an unlikely one, yet 'California Gurls' was a tearaway success. The summer anthem spent six weeks at No. 1 in the US, and broke the record for most weekly plays in the 17-year history of *Billboard*'s pop songs radio airplay chart.

The light-hearted ditty talks of the lure of Californian girls in their 'Daisy Dukes, bikinis on top'. The video is set in Candyland with the same vibrant colours and edible theme

'MTV was blocked from our house.'

Katy's sister Angela

'I couldn't wait to meet Katy Perry and then she came into the company shortly thereafter. She came flying into my office, did a cartwheel and was like, "Hi, I'm Katy Perry," and I was just mesmerized by her.'

Bob Semanovich, former Columbia Records marketing executive

'All of a sudden, things didn't work out with Island Def Jam. I didn't have money to pay for my car and I like, kept saying "I'm gonna get a record deal, I'm gonna get a record deal. I sounded like a broken record. And nobody believed me."'

Katy Perry

similar to the set of the Dreams tour. A cross between Willy Wonka's Chocolate Factory, Narnia and *Alice in Wonderland*, the video is a complete candy-coated indulgence, featuring Snoop in a special 'candy' suit and a walking army of real-life, giant gummy bears.

Perry defeats them at the end of the clip by shooting streams of whipped cream from cans attached to her bra – this was Perry's own idea. Giant lollipops, girls wrapped up in cellophane like chocolates and Katy pictured naked on her pink cloud with blue wig complete the indulgent dreamlike fantasy.

Explosive Imagination

Perry's award-winning video for the inspiring and catchy track 'Firework' is a departure from her usual style, portraying the singer in a more serious light – albeit with fireworks exploding from her chest. Directed by Dave Meyers, shooting involved an open casting call in Budapest, which attracted a record 38,000 applicants. Production of the video was part of a cross-promotional activity between Perry and Deutsche Telekom.

The video for single 'E.T' featuring Kanye West sees Perry transform from a glowing blue alien to a sci-fi golden gladiator while West raps in a spacepod. The big-budget supernatural video directed by Floria Sigismondi also features footage of gazelles, robots and an abandoned planet.

Joining Forces

Early collaborations with Glen Ballard, from the Island Records days, included 'Box', 'Diamonds' and 'Long Shot'. The singles were released on Perry's official Myspace page. Perry features as a backing vocalist on Gavin Rossdale's 2008 release *Wanderlust*. During her 'Hello Katy' Tour in 2009, material Perry recorded with The Matrix when signed to Columbia was released via a self-titled album on their in-house label, Let's Hear It.

Perry's vocals also feature on a remix of Colorado band 3OH!3's track 'Starstrukk'. The track was released on iTunes in August 2009. Perry had featured the band as a support act for part of her first solo tour, and the idea to collaborate sprang from there. Perry can also be heard on the fourth single from Timbaland's album, *Shock Value II*, which was released in December the same year. A live album of an MTV Unplugged performance by Perry was released in November 2009 and includes two new tracks. Missy Elliot has made a remix of Perry's track 'Last Friday Night (T.G.I.F.)'.

'I was just like, trying to live the life, I was trying to keep up with the Joneses because I wanted people to see me as someone they could really believe in.' Katy Perry

Style Icon

Perry has become almost as well known for her eye-popping outfits as she is for her hits. She says she likes to look like 'a history book'. She particularly favours the vintage 1940s look. Her playful, retro sense of style with a burlesque edge and Japanese schoolgirl twist has seen her top several best-dressed lists. Perry can also pull off sophistication with ease.

She adores bright colours and sequins, and is often photographed in whimsical pieces that play up her fun-loving personality. Some of her more memorable outfits include a tutu covered in multicoloured cupcakes, and a blinking, light-up dress. Perry's quirky style has an element of risk-taking to it. Her sense of style, although outlandish, rarely lets her down: her bold fashion choices have the added benefit of ensuring the press never tire of photographing her.

'I'm attracted to big personality anything, which usually means my clothes have a personality of their own. I like to not take it so seriously.'

Katy Perry

Girly Girl

Perry is a self-described 'girly girl' and is as obsessed with personal grooming as she is with fashion. She hates to be seen without makeup, which can take two hours to apply. Perry says she 'doesn't feel pretty' without the layers of slap, although claims her confidence is improving thanks to hubby Brand, who she says has 'taught me a lot about inner beauty'. Still, she wasn't impressed when he posted a snap of her 'sans makeup' on Twitter. Needless to say, it was quickly removed.

When it comes to her hair, Perry loves pushing boundaries and reinventing herself. She has performed in a multitude of crazy-coloured wigs and in 2011 her actual hair colour changed from brunette to red, to blond to pink, to a crazy shade of mauve within a few months. At the MTV Music Video Awards in 2011, Perry changed her nail art three times to match her outfits. The most elaborate look featured white and black checks, with each nail bed also displaying a different image.

Kooky Fruity Fun

During a performance at the 2009 Grammy Awards, Perry was lowered from the ceiling in a huge banana. That this feat had long been a 'dream' of hers highlights Perry's bizarre love of fruit. She loves fruit-shaped accessories and props, and seems to particularly favour strawberries, bananas, cherries

'I ordered a special chair from the dentist so I can lie back and *wake up* looking like a million bucks – I call it my Sleeping Beauty makeup.'

Katy Perry

'Besides my big boobs, it is probably my hourglass shape that is my best feature. I play off that a lot. I like that I have a lot on top and a lot on the bottom.'

Katy Perry

and watermelons. She has worn a glittering sequined fruit dress, often sports watermelon accessories and during her 'Hello Katy' Tour threw gigantic blow-up strawberries into the audience. She also loves other bizarre props, and has sung from within a giant high-heeled shoe and from the top of a huge pair of cherries. She also has a 'mascot', a giant lilac cat she calls 'Kitty Purry' after her own pet.

Body Image

While her curvaceous hourglass figure is admired the world over, Perry didn't always feel comfortable with her shape and has spoken openly of struggles with body image while still a teenager. An early bloomer, she was taunted by classmates and has revealed the hurt caused when she was nicknamed 'over the shoulder boulder holder' in the sixth grade. The teasing she endured prompted her to take the drastic action of taping her breasts to make them appear smaller, right up until the age of 19.

Now more than comfortable with her voluptuous shape, she prefers to highlight her curves instead of hiding them, playing up the sex kitten look in cleavage-enhancing bustiers and corsets, tiny playsuits and hotpants. Perry topped the *Maxim* Hot 100 Women in 2010. Former *Maxim* editor Joe Levy mused of her appeal: 'It's that feeling you get when you suddenly realize that the smartest, funniest, coolest girl you know also happens to be the best-looking and a pretty good skateboarder too. All of a sudden your crush goes supernova.'

'*I think* on some *level*
Katy was too original.
No one particularly *got*
Katy Perry
at that moment.'

Glen Ballard

Queen of Social

Perry is often described as a 'Twitter pioneer'. The micro-blogging site has played a significant role in promoting her profile and star power. Perry seems to be addicted to Twitter. She knows exactly how to make it work for her, chattering constantly and candidly about touring and travelling; bigging up and shouting out conspicuously to fellow celebrities and posting funny pictures and posts on her account. Very rarely does a day go by without at least one 'tweet' out of Perry.

An early Twitter convert, by August 2011 the star had 10 million followers, compared with just 3 million a year prior. Only Lady Gaga and Justin Bieber are more popular. Perry uses Twitter primarily for self-promotion. In October 2011, for example, she announced via Twitter that she would be releasing a new perfume and launched a competition for followers to guess what she had called it. The answer: Meow.

'She is so sweet. I can't wait to reveal her. Sweet dreams and pink ice creams, kittens!'

Katy Perry tweets about her new perfume.

Child of the Internet

In January 2011, Perry made a high-profile visit to Facebook headquarters, where she hung out with Mark Zuckerberg and announced North American dates for her California Dreams Tour. The announcement was made using Facebook Live. She let fans know they could use Facebook Places to check in to her tour venues and win prizes. Perry has over 35 million Facebook fans.

Her latest shows allow fans to post comments via Facebook Live or Twitter to a special account from where comments and feedback from the performance may be chosen to be posted on giant screens during the event. That's taking fan interaction to a truly different level. A contest on Facebook to promote the launch of Perry's first fragrance, Purr, saw the star's 'likes' shoot up over 400 per cent.

Blog-tastic

Perry also has a busy YouTube channel. She is excellent at self-publishing, and constantly posts short teasers before a single is released, or keeps fans interested by taking them on virtual backstage tours and responding to their questions in short video format. Perry's Myspace page was a big launch pad in her early days and still exists, while Perry has a blog on Tumblr that dates back to February 2008. Also reachable via a 'Dear Diary' link from her official site, the blog was started before 'I Kissed a Girl' was released and

'I love the Internet and social networking. I am a child of the Internet and am indebted to it.'

Katy Perry

'I thought to myself, "wow, I have written probably fifty odd songs now, I have met everyone in town, you know, my Rolodex is filled to the brim with numbers, so why isn't this happening?"'

Katy Perry

includes footage of Perry hearing herself on the radio for the first time. Other social media platforms used by Perry include Vimeo and Spotify. An official Katy Perry mobile application was launched in June 2011.

Kathy Beth Terry

Who is Kathy Beth Terry? Only Perry's hilarious online alter ego. She was initially created to generate a buzz surrounding the fifth single from *Teenage Dream*, 'Last Friday Night (T.G.I.F)', which features Kathy Beth Terry, a 13-year-old geeky girl with braces and glasses who apparently has no friends but likes to party with the best of them. Videos of Perry hamming it up as Kathy were an instant sensation. A 35-second trailer released as a teaser to the video of the song features Kathy Beth Terry looking at an invite on her corkboard to 'the party of the summer' before looking confused and asking herself: 'What, what was last night?' A flashback montage kicks in, showing wild festivities including dancing and Kathy puking into a shoe.

Kathy Beth Terry has taken on a life of her own with Facebook and Twitter accounts. Formerly friendless Kathy attracted an incredible 10,000 followers five hours after her first ever 'tweet'. Her profile says she loves Sudoku, Skip-it and Jonathan Taylor Thomas (JTT), and she loves science fairs and computer hacking.

Family Matters

Katy's relationship with her parents is intriguing, not least because of the way it has played out in public over recent years. Some media reports suggest a major falling out over Katy's sexy image. Perry claims they simply 'agree to disagree', and the approach works just fine.

What is certain is Keith and Mary Hudson are clearly not the types to shun the spotlight. While Keith initially declared his ministry 'over' when 'I Kissed a Girl' was released, in reality Katy's stardom has been good for drumming up interest in the couple's sermons and books. Keith, while freely admitting he was at first shocked by Katy's transformation from gospel girl to latex-clad pop princess, even adopted 'I Kissed God – and I liked it' as his tagline.

'*Sometimes when children grow up, their parents grow up. Mine grew up with me. We coexist. I don't try to change them any more and I don't think they try to change me.*'

Katy Perry

Gym Class Hero?

Perry has spoken openly about finding inspiration for her lyrics from past relationships. She has said the song 'Ur So Gay' refers to an 'emo' image-obsessed ex-boyfriend, while 'Hot n Cold' also refers to an ex. Only two former boyfriends, before Brand, have ever been identified. She was first linked to Matt Thiessen, lead singer in Christian band Reliant K, before meeting Travie McCoy, a fellow vocalist and the frontman of alternative hip-hop band Gym Class Heroes, at a New York recording studio in 2006. Although McCoy gave the young starlet a 'promise ring' they broke up in December 2008, before attempting to rekindle the romance briefly and unsuccessfully the following year.

The tumultuous relationship was relived in the press in 2010 following the release of Perry's song 'Circle the Drain', in which she sings about the failure of a relationship due to the other person's drug addiction. McCoy has spoken openly about opiate addiction and has spent two stints in rehab. Despite talking about the taste of a girl's cherry chapstick in her hit song 'I Kissed a Girl', Katy is not bisexual, although she admits having kissed a girl once when she was 19.

Russell Brand

Perry met Russell Brand while filming a cameo in his hit film *Get Him to the Greek* (2010). She filmed a kissing scene with him, although it was later deleted. They next ran into one another at the 2009 VMA Awards; he was hosting, she was performing. The chemistry between the all-American pop starlet and the bad boy British comedian was palpable.

'He's very *romantic*. We both are. From the beginning, I was *telepathically* telling him to *marry me*. From our *first dinner date*, I just knew he was *someone* who was going to be doing *great things*, and I wanted to *stand* by his side while it *happened*.'

Katy Perry

'The thing that attracts me to Russell, other than his gorgeous Samson hair, is his light, his energy, his constant search, drive, ambition.'

Katy Perry

The pair enjoyed a whirlwind four-month romance that Perry says 'felt like it was a movie' before Brand popped the question with a £30,000 Cartier gold and diamond ring. The media and public were at first cynical at the fast-moving relationship between the pastor's daughter and notorious former sex and heroin addict. Perry herself says she never has doubts about her 'Rusty Braunstein'. She describes him as sensitive, sweet, lovely and emotional, and told *Rolling Stone*: 'Russell has really made me more stable. I'm burning at such an incredible speed that I need someone stronger than me.'

The Wedding

The couple were married in a traditional ceremony in Rajasthan, India, the same place they got engaged, just two days before Perry's 26th birthday. Eighty guests were treated to a week-long stay in the exclusive Aman-I-Khas resort. Great lengths were taken to keep details of the wedding under wraps. Perry even announced to her followers she was taking a 'Twit Break' and wanted 'respect and privacy'. The tweetaholic couldn't stay away for long, posting a single photograph only a day after the ceremony with the caption 'WE DID'.

'Heartache to me is the easiest subject to write about. It's full of passion and feeling and everyone can relate.' *Katy Perry*

More Than A Songbird

Perry's biggest coup as far as the big screen goes is landing the role of Smurfette – or rather the voice of Smurfette – in *The Smurfs* movie (2011). She cemented her star status playing a yellow version of herself on *The Simpsons Christmas Special* (2010) and also played herself in an episode of *The Young and the Restless*. She put in a cameo appearance as Honey in the hit comedy *How I Met Your Mother*.

In 2010, Perry recorded a video of a performance of 'Hot n Cold' with Elmo from *Sesame Street*. The segment was axed before airing due to concerns that Perry's dress showed too much cleavage. The video has been posted to YouTube. A cameo scene featuring her kissing her future husband, Russell Brand, in *Get Him to the Greek*, never made it to air either. Perry claims it was deleted due to the producer's concerns that subsequent interest in the pair's real-life relationship would detract from the film.

Katy Perry Trivia

Perry says she can't cook, but adores cleaning. She has a 'Jesus' tattoo on her wrist, to remind her where she comes from. She loves garage sales, and her dad still wakes her up at 7 am at weekends when she is at home to go bargain hunting. She is a fan of skating, both on land and on ice.

'In my old place I used to schedule my housekeeper at times when I could clean too, and we would clean together. It got to the point where I needed things in the fridge to point a certain way.'

Katy Perry

'Sometimes the things you want to happen in your life don't happen on your schedule, because it's all about timing. Rejection was God's projection.'

Katy Perry

A cat lover, she and Russell have three cats together, Kitty Purry, Katy's original cat, Russell's 'English cat' Morrissey and their new pussy, Krusty.

The Perry Legacy

She is friendly with celebrity blogger Perez Hilton. She loves mini golf. She hops like a bunny when she is happy, such as when she finished filming the scene with Brand in *Get Him to the Greek*. She first told Russell she loved him by hiring an aeroplane trailing the proclamation conspicuously through the sky. She wants her ashes shot out over the California coast in a firework. Her natural hair colour is dirty blonde.

Angelica Cob-Baehler, the former Columbia executive who helped get Perry her eventual deal with Capitol, says the singer will leave a legacy. 'Her legacy will probably be about how she inspired people to be themselves. How she inspired people to not take life so seriously, how she took hard knocks and turned them into positives and never gave up on her dream.'

'I couldn't believe how good she was. I knew I was encountering talent in capital letters. I knew she was a star.' Glen Ballard

'At age forty-five ...
I'll look back on this journey
and I'll be like, "oh yeah,
I have learned some things,
I've learned some lessons."
I'll have some stories to tell,
hopefully. I'll leave my
fingerprint on the world.'

Katy Perry

Further Information

Katy Perry Vital Info

Birth Name Katheryn Elizabeth Hudson

Birth Date 25 October 1984

Birth Place Santa Barbara, CA

Height 1.72 m (5 ft 8 in)

Nationality American

Alter Ego Kathy Beth Terry

Discography

Albums & EPs

Katy Hudson (2001)

Ur So Gay (EP, 2007)

One of the Boys (2008)

The Hello Katy Australian Tour EP (EP, 2009)

MTV Unplugged (2009)

Teenage Dream (2010)

Singles

2007: 'Ur So Gay'

2008: 'I Kissed a Girl' (No. 1)

'Hot n Cold' (No. 1)

2009: 'Thinking of You'

'Waking Up in Vegas'

'Starstrukk' (3OH!3 feat. Katy Perry)

2010: 'If We Ever Meet Again' (Timbaland feat. Katy Perry)

'California Gurls' (feat. Snoop Dogg, No. 1)

'Teenage Dream' (No. 1)

'Firework' (No. 1)

2011: 'E.T.' (feat. Kanye West, US No. 1)

'Last Friday Night (T.G.I.F)' (No. 1)

'The One That Got Away'

Awards

Billboard Music Awards

2011: Top Hot 100 Artist

Top Digital Songs Artist

BMI Awards

2011: Award Winning Song ('California Gurls')

BRIT Awards

2009: International Female Artist

Cosmopolitan Ultimate Women Of The Year Awards

2010: Ultimate Star International Music

Maxim Magazine Award

2010: Sexiest Woman In The World

MTV Awards

2008: Best New Act (MTV Europe)

2009: Best Ringtone ('Hot n Cold', Los Premios

MTV Latinoamérica)

Best Breakthrough (MTV Australia)

Best Pop Video ('I Kissed a Girl', Video

Music Awards Japan)

2010: Best Video ('California Gurls', MTV Europe)

2011: Video of the Year ('Firework', Video Music Awards)

Best Collaboration ('E.T.', feat Kanye West,

Video Music Awards)

Best Special Effects ('E.T.', Video Music Awards)

MP3 Music Awards

2010: The MIC Award (Music Industry Choice,

'California Gurls')

Nickelodeon Kids' Choice Awards

2010: Fave Song ('California Gurls', Australian

Kids' Choice)

2011: Favourite Female Singer (American Kids' Choice)

Fave International Artist (Australian Kids' Choice)

Best International Song ('Firework', Mexican

Kids' Choice)

People's Choice Awards

2009: Favourite Pop Song ('I Kissed a Girl')

2011: Favourite Female Artist

Favourite Internet Sensation

Teen Choice Awards

2010: Choice Music: Single ('California Gurls')

Choice Summer: Song ('California Gurls')

2011: Choice Summer: Female Artist

Choice Music: Tour (California Dreams Tour)

VH1 Awards

2011: Song of the Summer ('Last Friday Night')

Online

katyperry.com:

Official site with news, tour diary and photos

katy-perry.org:

News, videos, posts, fun and more

myspace.com/katyperry:

Check this site out for Katy Perry's latest songs, videos and tour updates

facebook.com/katyperry:

Check out twitter.com/katyperry for Katy P's latest writing on the wall: Join the 12 million other followers at @katyperry

Biographies

Alice Hudson (Author)

From New Zealand, Alice fused twin passions for writing and music while a student, reviewing and interviewing international bands and DJs. She is currently based in London, writing and researching for corporate clients across a wide range of sectors, from health and fitness and financial services, to social media and entertainment.

Mango Saul (Foreword)

Mango Saul has been a music, lifestyle and entertainment journalist for ten years. Some of his highlights include having breakfast at Waffle House with rapper Ludacris in Atlanta, sharing a bed with Destiny's Child for a *Smash Hits* cover interview and being sent an ice-cream costume for no reason. As editor of Sugarscape.com, Mango has seen the site grow to over 4 million page views per month and was shortlisted for Digital Editorial Individual 2011 at the AOP Awards.

Picture Credits

All images © Getty Images:

Tony Barson/WireImage: 22; Bryan Bedder: 112; Michael Buckner/WireImage: 94; Gustavo Caballero: 64; Michael Caulfield/WireImage: 28; Victor Chavez/WireImage: 43; Lester Cohen/WireImage: 29; Jemal Countess: 51; Marcos Delgado/Clasos.com/LatinContent: 102; Charles Eshelman/FilmMagic: 58; Shirlaine Forrest/WireImage: 4, 10, 52; Ian Gavan: 127; Ross Gilmore/Redferns: 18; Steve Granitz/WireImage: 101; Samir Hussein: 110; Dimitrios Kambouris/WireImage: 24; Jeff Kravitz/FilmMagic: 7, 33, 85, 91, 98, 105, 106; Steffen Kugler: 74; Bob Levey/WireImage: 117; Neil Lupin: 124; Eamonn McCormack/WireImage: 8; Martin McNeil/WireImage: 107; Kevin Mazur/WireImage: 12, 56, 65, 66, 68, 88, 118, 122; Mike Marsland: 109; Mike Marsland/WireImage: 114; Buda Mendes/LatinContent: 76; Buda Mendes/STF/LatinContent: 26, 120; Jason Merritt/FilmMagic: 21, 38; George Napolitano/FilmMagic: 73; John Parra/FilmMagic: 62; Martin Philbey/Redferns: 70; Ryan Pierse: 61; George Pimentel/WireImage: 35, 44, 46; Chris Polk/FilmMagic: 30; Christopher Polk: 78; Alberto E. Rodriguez: 96; Ferdaus Shamim: WireImage: 87; John Shearer/ WireImage: 40; Amy Sussman: 49; Michael Tran/FilmMagic: 54; Greetsia Tent/WireImage: 14; Noel Vasquez: 16; Theo Wargo/WireImage: 82, 93; Katy Winn: 80